The Heart and Soul of Me

Nicole Clark

Presentation by *BookLeaf Publishing*

Web: www.bookleafpub.com

E-mail: info@bookleafpub.com

ISBN: 9789357742382

First edition 2023

Passion

1

Love is passion we all need to feel.
Love is has the power we all need to heal.
Earth is a place which love exists so painfully.
We all need to see, that only that you have the
power to comfort thee.

Racing the Wind

Gliding swiftly across the Earth, building my
pride for all it's worth.
Racing the wind, I am up to a tie- to all my tears,
I say goodbye.
I am determined, there is no quitting, there is no
giving.
For my life has just been born and I am now just
living.
All my joy, all my fears, all my love condensed
into so many years.
I will win against the wind. The race will be
long-I will not give in.
If you find yourself losing the race and and the
end is by your side-put your hand on your heart
and know your worth-build up your pride.
The race is yours to win. Losing, will be a sin.

Obsession

I have an obsession. An obsession with love. The feeling is too great, like the flight of a dove. I used to see love as a storybook romance that never went wrong. Now, I see it in our children's eyes, I hear it in a song.

I have an obsession for your long embrace. The warmth from your love puts a smile on my face. I want to feel that warmth, I want to smile all of the time. I want you to have that obsession too, but you do not. It is all mine.

Passion and courting all die out too quick. It is the love from a hug, laughter and tears; those are things that apparently stick. It turns out there is no storybook romance in real life-but if you stop and look around it can be even better- just building a home, raising a family as husband and wife.

Forever to Be

Right now you do not know me or my hopes and dreams and fears. I think of not being with you and it brings my eyes to tears.
I long to know how you think, and what you dream of at night. What could it be? Are we wrong or are we right?
I dream of a soft whispered wind, sweet smelling flowers and sharing things that we call ours.
Warmth to heat up my cold and icy body, a melody to bring me happiness, rather than melancholy.
All these things remind me of something sweeter and strong and true. All of these things, remind me of you.

Caught up on you

5

You give a feeling I've never felt before. You give me confusion, and I never feel sure.
If only you could love me, the way that I love you, I can make you happy. I can make all of your dreams come true.
The peaceful sounds of whispers in my ear-for only when I am with you it is my mind and body I want to share.
On a cold and reckless night, my heart and mind puts up a fight. My heart tells me yes, my mind tells me no. Yet I hold on. We built too much for me to go.

The Deserving

Nobody needs love more than someone who
doesn't deserve it.
If we wait for people to become lovable before
we love them, we will wait forever.
It is precisely in being loved that we become
lovable.

Alone No More

For I stand alone, empty inside. Everything I
feel runs rapidly through my mind.
For I am alone with no one to comfort my pain. I
am standing alone in the rain.
For all it's worth, my pain and happiness lingers
on old and new-alone, empty and blue.
But I pick myself up and remind myself of the
lives I created and nurtured so true.
As long as I have them, I am never alone or
scared. The love I have for them and the strength
they give me, can never be compared.

Golden Heaven

As I awake to a pinkish-golden sunrise, I see the beauty and majesty that our mother did comprise. Birds are singing their morning songs and the dew on the grass sparkles and shimmers. The glow from the sunrise, peeks through the trees and their silhouettes glimmer.
The grows long and the wind blows strong, the fresh air fills your soul with peace and contentment.
Animals frolic throughout the lush green, life passes us by slowly, our worries unseen.
As dusk falls upon us, and the sky becomes golden and pink once more, and the moon begins to shine. Stars peek out in the night sky, all of the wishes are mine.
Fireflies glow and the air becomes cooler. Our Mothers love is a golden heaven. Nothing is truer.

Beautiful

When you were born with the soul of an angel,
born with the stars in your eyes and roses melted
into your lips and skin so soft you would swear
it was made from silk; that is aesthetic beauty.
When you are born with a mind in constant
search of all that is true and wisdom in your
heart and a passion for justice and kindness to
all; that is true beauty.

Forever by Your Side

Since the first time I saw you, my eyes couldn't believe; two angels I have received. You bring me such love and joy, I cannot hide. You my loves, I am forever by your side.

Two souls made from love within my body offer me comfort and pride. When they come into the world and I see their eyes, all I can do is smile and cry tears of happiness.

Your fingers are so tiny, your faces so perfect. I comfort you both with a mother's embrace and caress.

As you grow older and distant and develop strong pride, just know that I will always love you and will be forever by your side.

Angel

I hence forth to bow upon your body of non-existence. I weep my tears, I suffer my pain I see an angel appear before me, and fear I have to gain.

Grassy colored eyes shed much sorrow, for he can be no more, there is no tomorrow. He reaches his hand into mine and and whispers words of comfort and sorrow- and the glow ceases to shine.

The angel says that heaven is waiting and he must go. I beg to go with him, but he says it's not my time, the answer is no.

The angel says I will live on in your heart and in your mind. When your time comes to go to heaven, it is you I will find.

Future Shadows of My Past

I traveled to my future, and watched myself
grow old.
I pondered my past as my soul grew cold.
My mind was blank and I had confusion to
thank.
For what shall I say when I look back on this
very day?
Will I look back and despise myself for what I
have done?
Or will I chuckle at the risky fun?
I stood there and stared at my older self in time,
while my soul so ever recklessly was hypnotized
by my prime.

We All Need Love

What is love?
Love is sharing our laughter, sharing our pain.
Love is forgiving and dancing in the rain.
If we all could show it, maybe every person could know it.
Until that day we all will have to live with what we've got. Not all of us can experience it, but surely our tender hearts all need it whether we want it or not.
We all need love like we need air.
The feeling of love is so great-there is nothing to compare.

I Love You

I love you.
Not just for what you are, but how you make me
feel.
So charming and delightful, you are my best
deal.
I love you.
A beauty like you is loved by many everyday.
But I have more love for you, and any
consequence I will pay.
I love you.
You hold me so tight, caress me just right, we
lay in each others arms, all through the night.
I love you.
You are the most special person I have ever
known. When I first laid eyes on you, heaven
had shone.
I love you.
I wish for our love to last eternally. No one has a
stronger love than you and me.

A Simple Thought

Life is beauty, life is pain.
Life is growth from the rain.
Life can offer challenges and despair.
Life can offer beauty so fair.
Life is simple, if you do not complicate.
Life is demanding, but you must find the
beautiful in the chaos.
Life is meant to be savored in all we have gained
and lost.

Love in Young and Old

Time carries on and a passionate kiss is a desire.
My heart will melt, and my body heats up like fire.
When we were in our youth, passion was never-ending and we were on top of the world.
Now life has caught up to us. Our bodies that once were tangled in each other now grow tired and old.
We found a new kind of passion in building our home, laughing and keeping each other warm in the cold.
We may not be the fiery lovers we once were-but stronger in our love now, knowing each others minds-for that I am sure.

My Forever Valentine

The first time that I saw you, a shiver went up my spine. I fell in love and prayed to God that you would soon be mine.
You said you loved and my prayers were answered one fateful day.
My words were muted, there was not much I could say.
Since then we never left each others sides and built a life so fine.
I love you now, I love you still, my forever Valentine.

Love is Forever

I will love you tomorrow, like I still do today.
If you grow to not feel the same, I will still love
you anyway.
All of the pain is forgotten, all of the hurt is
forgiven.
Without you and our family, I could not go on
living.
We have had laughter and carefree happiness.
We have been through pain and suffering, but
loving each other with our best.
We raised our beautiful children with love and
guidance and care.
For all we have been through, I know, it is
eternity with you I want to share.

Printed in the USA
CPSIA information can be obtained
at www.ICGtesting.com
LVHW041211310124
770460LV00065B/1625